HEALED *from the* BONDAGE *of* MY PAST

The Pivot that Saved My Life

A Memoir by

Dr. Kimberly Lowe

Copyright © 2025 Dr. Kimberly Lowe. All rights reserved.

Dedication

☙

To the little girl I used to be—

Who carried silence like a secret and pain like a badge.

You survived what should have crushed you.

This book is proof that your voice was never lost—it was just waiting for healing.

To the grown woman I am today—

I'm so very proud of you, let's go higher!

To the women still in their wilderness—

May these words be a hand reaching back to pull you forward.

You are not too late. You are not too broken. You are not alone.

Let this be your pivot.

To my spiritual parents Johnathan & Jessica (Moma J) Davis—

Thank you for covering me, teaching me and correcting me during the lowest points in my life. It was your sound wisdom and voice that started my pivot.

To my support system—

The intercessors, encouragers, and truth-tellers who prayed, checked in, and stood watch while I healed. You know who you are and you remain my secret weapons.

Your love held me together when I wanted to fall apart. Thank you for seeing me whole even before I believed I could be.

And above all—

To my Father, my Redeemer, my Healer.

Every word in this book exists because of You.

You turned my mourning into dancing, my shame into testimony, my bondage into ministry.

May this offering bring You glory, and may every reader feel Your presence in these pages.

TABLE OF CONTENTS

Chapter 1: **Root of Bondage**

Chapter 2: **When Love Becomes a Lie**

Chapter 3: **Numb But Functioning**

Chapter 4: **The Silence Behind the Smile**

Chapter 5: **When Grief Shattered My World**

Chapter 6: **Where Healing Began**

Chapter 7: **Forgiveness Ain't Weakness**

Chapter 8: **The Woman in the Mirror**

Chapter 9: **From Wound to Weapon**

Chapter 10: **I'm Not Who I Was**

INTRODUCTION

☙

I almost didn't write this book.

Not because I didn't have something to say—but because I wasn't sure I was worth listening to. I've carried pain so long it started to feel like part of my identity. I was/am the strong one, the "smile-through-it" kind, the "keep-pushing" kind, and yet, inside, I was suffocating under the weight of wounds I never gave language to.

Healed from the Bondage of My Past isn't a story wrapped in a pretty bow. This is a book about bondage, about heartbreak, about healing. It's about the nights I cried out to God with no words, just groans. And it's about the moment He whispered back, *"I've been waiting for you to hand it over."*

There's a version of me that use to beg for love. Settle for less. Keep silent to keep peace. But God didn't leave me in the cycle. He disrupted it—with grace, not guilt. With clarity, not chaos.

This book is for the woman still hiding behind her strength. For the one who learned how to function but forgot how to feel. For the one who's tired of surviving and ready to live. If you've ever questioned your worth, your purpose, or whether you'd ever be whole again—this is for you.

Each chapter is layered with truth. Some pages might sting; others will soothe. You'll find journaling prompts, scriptures, and personal stories that show healing isn't linear—but it is possible. This isn't just my testimony—it's a mirror. A map. A movement.

You don't have to stay stuck.

You don't have to stay small.

You don't have to stay silent.

Let this be your moment to pivot. Not perfectly, but powerfully. Not overnight, but over time—with God guiding every step.

Let's do this together.

Chapter 1: Root of Bondage

When Innocence Met Silence

Childhood Innocence

☙

My earliest childhood memory takes me back to when I was about five years old. Across the street from our house sat a small park. I loved going there, not just for the swings or slides, but for the friends I met there.

These friends were invisible to everyone else, but they were very real to me. We talked with each other, and their presence brought me comfort and joy in ways I couldn't explain. For years, I didn't understand who they were—I only knew they were mine.

It wasn't until much later in life that I realized they weren't imaginary at all. They were angels. God had already stationed them around me, introducing me to His presence before I even had the words to name it. At five years old, I was already beginning to dream, to see visions, and to sense God in ways far beyond my age. Heaven was marking me early.

But the enemy is never idle when God's hand is evident in life.

☙

The Memory That Changed Everything

By the age of eight or nine, a darker memory took root. I was at a relative's house when I experienced something no child should ever have to endure—I was touched in ways that broke my innocence and safety. I remember being made to lie on the bed and open my legs. He asked if anyone else had ever touched me there before. Shaking, I whispered no.

My no stopped him that day, but the experience left me confused and broken. I never felt comfortable or safe at that particular family member's house again. Each time I saw him, I was reminded of that night—but I never told a soul. That moment also unearthed an even earlier childhood memory I had buried deep inside—being touched by another trusted adult relative.

A couple of years later, another violation occurred at a different family member's home. But this time, I wasn't alone. Other young female relatives carried the same unspoken pain. We never said a word to each other, but we knew. We knew because no one wanted to be left alone with that particular male relative at night. Without ever having a conversation, we all shared the same silent understanding: this wasn't safe. This wasn't right.

And from that day, I learned an unspoken rule that shaped much of my life: Never Tell.

༄

The Root of Bondage

Looking back, I understand why I felt such tension between those two memories. At five years old, God began revealing Himself to me through angels, dreams, and visions. His Spirit touched my life early. But by nine, the enemy launched his counterattack.

That incident planted seeds of secrecy, shame, and fear. Those seeds grew deep roots that would take me over forty years to confront and overcome.

That was the root of bondage—the moment silence became my survival mechanism. The moment the enemy tried to choke out the calling God had planted in me by making me afraid of my own truth.

From that day forward, I carried a silent battle: the light of God pulling me toward freedom, and the darkness of trauma pulling me toward captivity.

Reflection

I share this not to glorify pain, but to reveal the truth: the roots of bondage grow in silence. What we don't confront, we carry. And what we carry in silence can become chains.

John 8:32 reminds us, *"You shall know the truth, and the truth shall make you free."* The first step to freedom is acknowledging the truth, even when it hurts. Silence may feel safe, but it only keeps us bound. Freedom comes when we dare to tell the truth—first to God, and then to ourselves.

What began as an unseen root soon showed itself in how I lived—smiling on the outside while suffocating in silence within.

Time to Journal

☙

What moments in your early life shaped the way you view love, safety, and identity?

_____
_____
_____
_____
_____
_____
_____
_____
_____
_____
_____
_____
_____
_____
_____
_____
_____

Healed from the Bondage of My Past: The Pivot that Saved My Life

Closing Prayer

☙

Lord, thank You for being present in both my innocence and my pain. Even in moments I didn't understand, You were there. I pray for the courage to tell the truth about my story, knowing that Your truth is what brings freedom. Heal the places in me where silence once ruled and let Your light rewrite the narrative of my life. In Jesus' name, Amen.

☙

Affirmation

The root of bondage no longer defines me. God's truth exposes silence, uproots fear, and leads me into freedom.

Chapter 2: When Love Becomes a Lie

Breaking Free from False Definitions of Love

The Ache That Started Early

☙

I came into the world already carrying a wound I didn't understand. Taken from my mother almost at birth, I was separated from the one person who was supposed to be my first safe place. Even before I had language, my spirit registered the loss. The absence and knowing I had a biological mother somewhere left me hungering for something I couldn't name but would spend years chasing.

My biological father gave me to the only mother I knew for years, and she conditioned my mind to believe that my real mother didn't want anything to do with me. I carried that belief like a scar across my heart—silent, deep, and shaping the way I saw love. It wasn't until my biological mother, and I finally had the hard conversation in my adult hood that I learned the truth: she longed for me. She came back for me. She tried to take me home. But she was never allowed to.

And when I look back now, I understand that the emptiness I felt growing up wasn't imagined—it was inherited, it was a generational curse, and It was the echo of a separation I never should have experienced.

☙

The First Time I Saw Her ... Again

Before I ever knew the full story, before I could even understand the lies that shaped my childhood, there was one moment that stood out— a moment when God allowed me to reconnect to the bond that shattered at birth

I was still a little girl when I saw my mother again and met some of my siblings for the first time. My father took me to visit them in Mississippi. I was too young to understand the weight of the moment, but old enough to feel the shift in the atmosphere of my heart.

I remember the nervous flutter in my stomach, the way my small hands fidgeted, and how my breath felt tight in my chest. I didn't have the words for what I was feeling. But my spirit knew something important was happening.

And then I saw her.

My mother.

She was beautiful—quietly, powerfully beautiful. There was a softness in her eyes that made my young heart pause. Something in me recognized her, even if my mind didn't know how. It felt like a piece of me had suddenly been returned—a piece I didn't even know belonged to her. I wish I could have held on to her, telling her that I didn't want to go back, don't let me go back!

Then I saw my siblings.

Up until that day, I believed the only sibling I had was a sister on my father's side in Arkansas. That was my reality. That was all I knew. But suddenly, another sister stood in front of me—a sister and a brother who looked like me, smiled like me, and carried pieces of a story I didn't know I was part of.

I remember staring at my sister with wide eyes, trying to understand how someone who felt like a stranger could also feel like home. I was so happy to know I had another sister that loved me as much as I loved her and a brother that called me his other big sister.

Children don't think their way through moments like that—they feel their way through them.

And I felt everything:

Joy.

Relief.

Confusion.

And a strange sense of wholeness I didn't have a name for.

For the first time in my little life, I felt a kind of connection that didn't have to be explained. A kind that simply was.

That moment didn't erase the fractures in my childhood. It didn't magically fill the voids or untangle the confusion of my early years. But it settled something in me. It completed a piece of my identity—even if I didn't yet understand it. And just as quickly as that moment arrived, life pulled me back into the reality I had to survive.

The truth is- pain doesn't begin with the event you remember. It begins in the soil of the roots—the moments, the wounds, the absences, the secrets. And although meeting my mother and siblings offered me a glimpse of belonging, it didn't shield me from the storms that would shape my early years. My foundation was already cracked. My identity already questioned. My spirit already learning how to be strong because life wasn't giving me many other options.

But even still, God was there—quietly weaving pieces together that I didn't know needed to be healed. He was watching the roots, the rupture, and the restoration long before I could name what was happening to me.

And this is where my story truly begins:

Not at the moment I broke...

but at the moment life planted the seeds of bondage that I would spend years trying to understand.

This is the beginning of the unraveling.

The exposure.

The truth-telling.

The beginning of how I became who I was—before I ever knew who I would become.

And as painful as these roots are to revisit, they are necessary... because healing never starts at the branches.

It starts at the roots.

That hunger for love—for the love I lost too early—drove me into the arms of people who couldn't possibly fill what was missing. It made me crave affection, attention, and acceptance in ways that left me vulnerable. I didn't realize it then, but my life had been shaped by silence long before I understood its power.

Silence taught me to keep pain hidden.

Silence taught me to pretend I was okay.

Silence taught me to accept love in whatever form it showed up—even when it wasn't love at all.

Because when you've been separated from your first source of love, you spend years learning how to redefine it... often through trial, error, and heartbreak.

And for a long time, love became whatever lie I needed to believe just to feel whole.

Going back, I realized the emptiness; and that hunger that I desired drove me into the arms of people who couldn't possibly fill what was missing. It made me crave affection, attention, and acceptance in ways that often left me vulnerable. I didn't realize it then, but my life had been conditioned by silence—keeping pain tucked away so no one could see.

My First Boyfriend

❧

I was still a teenager when I thought I had found love for the first time. He was my boyfriend, my "first," and in my heart, that meant something. I wanted him to be the answer to the ache I carried inside. The butterflies, the late-night calls, the way he looked at me—it felt like the love I thought I deserved.

But it didn't take long for shadows to creep into the relationship. His jealousy, his anger, his need to control me—I overlooked it all because I was desperate for his presence. I told myself, *"At least someone wants me. At least I'm not alone."*

❧

The Day Everything Changed

One day, we got into a heated argument. I can't even remember what started it, but I will never forget how it ended. His eyes narrowed, his voice grew sharper, and before I could process what was happening, he grabbed me. Then he hit me.

For a split second, I froze. Then something in me rose up—I wasn't the type to just take it. I fought back because I was a fighter. But even as I swung, even as I tried to defend myself, my heart sank. This wasn't love.

What I didn't know in that moment was that our next-door neighbor had been watching. She saw what happened and later told my mom— the aunt who was raising me. That afternoon, when I got home from school, my mom confronted me.

Her words were firm: *"Did he put his hands on you?"*

My heart pounded. My throat tightened. Everything in me wanted to scream yes, but instead, I shook my head and said, *"No."*

Why? Because I had already learned the power of silence. I had learned to keep secrets, to bury the truth, to act like nothing ever happened. So, I lied, protecting him and hiding myself.

That lie became the beginning of not just verbal abuse, but physical abuse. Once the door was opened, the line was crossed again and again. So, relationship after relationship physical abuse became acceptable.

ଓ

Silence That Spoke Louder Than Words

I carried the shame in silence. No one knew. On the outside, I smiled, went to school, laughed with friends, but inside, I was bruised—physically, emotionally, and spiritually.

That silence became a prison. Each time I pretended nothing happened, I gave them more permission to hurt me. And each time I allowed it, my sense of worth slipped further away.

ଓ

The Mirage of Love

I convinced myself his anger was passion. His jealousy meant he cared. His control meant I was valuable. But what I called love was really bondage. It wasn't protection—it was possession.

The lies I believed shaped the way I saw myself: not enough, undeserving, replaceable. I thought love meant enduring pain, because I was too afraid to believe there could be more.

ଓ

Soul Ties That Chained Me

That first relationship created a soul tie that lingered even after it was over. I thought leaving him would mean freedom, but my spirit was still entangled. I replayed his words, his hands, his apologies that were only empty promises. I struggled to let go, even when I knew I should.

Toxic love is like quicksand—the harder you fight to stand upright in it without God, the deeper you sink.

☙

The Truth About Love

God had to reteach me what love really is. Love is patient and kind. Love protects. Love tells the truth. Love heals. Real love looks like Jesus.

It took time for me to understand that what I had experienced wasn't love at all. It was pain wearing a mask. It was the counterfeit. And counterfeits always cost more than they give. Unfortunately, I would continue to learn that the hard way.

Let's Journal

ଔ

Think back to your first experiences with love. What did they teach you—good or no bad? Were there moments you stayed silent when you should have spoken up? Write them out. Then ask yourself: what is the difference between what you experienced and what God says love truly is?

_____

_____

_____

_____

_____

_____

_____

_____

_____

_____

_____

_____

_____

_____

Closing Prayer

ങ

Father, I surrender every false definition of love I've carried. Heal the wounds left by abuse, lies, and silence. Break every soul tie that keeps me bound to relationships that were never Your will. Teach me to recognize and accept love that mirrors You—love that is kind, gentle, and pure. In Jesus' name, Amen.

ങ

Affirmation

I am no longer silent about my pain. I am no longer bound by counterfeit love. I am worthy of love that is patient, kind, and rooted in God's truth.

Chapter 3: Numb But Functioning

Dying to Live

The Mask of Strength

☙

Fast forward to many failed promiscuous relationships and I've now moved to Mississippi to escape my past and to reunite with my birth mother and siblings; only to dive deeper into a tangled web of heartbreak and relationships in which I thought were me being in love but ended up just being disappointment after disappointment. I eventually got into church and married. I married after only dating for eight months but this relationship was different. The toxicity that was in my previous relationships wasn't there, but we were nowhere near ready for marriage. I was nowhere near healed. He became a Pastor years later and now I'm attempting to survive in ministry. From the outside, I looked like the woman who had it all together. I was dependable, present, and always smiling. People would always count on me, inside and outside of the ministry. I never let on that behind the smile was a soul weighed down with sorrow, pain, and a silent ache I didn't have the courage to put into words.

Numbness became my shield. I wore it like armor. If I stayed busy — working, serving in church, taking care of everyone else — then maybe, just maybe, I wouldn't have to sit still long enough to feel the loneliness gnawing at me. My calendar was full of busy work, my phone never stopped buzzing, and yet my heart was empty.

I thought that strength meant never letting anyone see me cry. I thought that if I admitted how much I was hurting, I would be a burden. So, I put on my mask, polished my smile, and became the *"strong one"* for everyone else. I was fooling myself; I put on problem to the side and put on another one, masking the root with the branches.

The Silent Superwoman

☙

I can still see myself standing in the church hallway one Sunday morning, dressed to the nines. My hair was done, my heels clicked confidently on the floor, and my face carried that same practiced smile I had worn for years. To the outside world, I looked radiant. Inside, though, I felt like I was suffocating.

"Good morning! How are you?" one of the church parishioners asked patting my hand as she passed by.

I said lightly, *"I'm good!"*

But the truth was, I wasn't good. I was numb. I had cried in the shower that morning, wiping my tears quickly so I could apply my makeup. I had practiced my smile in the mirror, making sure it looked convincing. I had learned to silence the part of me that wanted to scream, *"I'm not okay!"*

After service, a friend pulled me aside. *"Kim, are you sure you're alright? You seem... tired."*

Again, I gave the answer I thought was safe. *"I'm fine. Just busy, you know how it is."*

And she nodded, satisfied, because I sounded strong. But when I got home and closed the door behind me, the smile fell. The weight of it all — the brokenness, the rejection, the loneliness — came crashing down. I curled up in my bed, staring at the ceiling, numb. Not angry, not even sad anymore. Just empty.

In that silence, I could almost hear God whisper:

"Daughter, you don't have to keep pretending. Come to Me. Bring Me your weariness. Lay down what you're carrying. I will give you rest."

For the first time, I let myself whisper back through tears: *"Lord, I'm tired. I can't carry this anymore."* And in that raw moment, I felt something shift a bit. His presence wrapped around me like a blanket, and I realized that being strong all the time wasn't what He wanted from me. He wanted me to lean on Him.

☙

The Truth About Numbing

Numbness is not the same as peace. Peace is a gift from God; numbness is a survival mechanism. One heals, the other hides. Numbing ourselves might keep us from feeling pain for a moment, but it also keeps us from experiencing joy, love, and the comfort of God's Spirit.

When Jesus calls us to, *"Come to Him,"* He is offering something better than strength through performance — He is offering rest through surrender. Rest doesn't mean weakness; it means trust. It means letting God carry what we cannot carry on our own. It wasn't until I could fully trust God that I would know what rest looked and felt like

As I look back on those years of smiling through the pain, I realize how much of my life was spent living for appearances instead of truth. Behind closed doors, my heart was still crying out for love (even though I was now married), for validation, and for something real. Living behind a mask of strength kept me from healing, but it also left me vulnerable. When your soul is numb, you crave love in any form that promises to make you feel alive again. That silent hunger can pull you into relationships that look like love but carry the power to wound even deeper. I'll explain more later.

Let's Journal

☙

In what ways did you numb your pain while appearing strong? What masks did you wear so others wouldn't see your brokenness? Write honestly about what you were afraid they might discover.

_____
_____
_____
_____
_____
_____
_____
_____
_____
_____
_____
_____
_____
_____
_____

Closing Prayer

೧೩

Father, I come before You weary and worn from carrying what was never mine to bear. For so long, I hid behind smiles, busyness, and strength that wasn't real. But today, I choose to lay down the mask. I choose to bring You my numbness, my silence, and my hidden pain. Lord, breathe life back into the places that feel empty. Restore my heart and teach me what it means to truly rest in You. Help me to recognize the people you have sent into my life to help me. Thank You for seeing me, loving me, and calling me to wholeness. In Jesus' name, Amen.

೧೩

Affirmation

I no longer have to perform to prove my strength. My rest is in God, and my healing begins when I surrender. I am seen, I am loved, and I am safe in His arms. I am Whole and Complete lacking and wanting nothing.

Chapter 4: The Silence Behind the Smile

The Mask Of Strength Can Hide Pain, But It Cannot Hide From God

The Mask of Strength

☙

I feel like people thought that I was always the strong one; some would even say to me that they didn't know how I did certain things.

I smiled politely when I heard those words, but inside I wanted to whisper back, *"If only you knew."*

People admired my strength, but what they really saw was my mask. My smile was not just an expression—it was armor. Every time I flashed it, I was hiding the storm that raged inside. I was hiding the pain, the disappointment, the resentment and the tears.

To the outside world, my laughter was genuine, my presence stable, my faith unshakable. But the truth? Behind that smile was a woman holding her breath, afraid that if she exhaled too deeply, all the pain she had buried would come rushing out.

☙

The Pressure to Perform

"Are you okay?" someone once asked me after church.

"I'm fine," I said quickly, pulling the corners of my mouth upward before they could look too closely.

But I wasn't fine. I was exhausted. I was tired of holding everything together, tired of feeling like the world expected me to be a pillar that never cracked.

The pressure to perform felt relentless. At work, I gave my best. At home, I carried the weight. At church, I wore the crown of strength. Everywhere I went, the silent rule was the same: **Don't fall apart. Don't let them see.**

The lies whispered constantly:

- *If they knew the truth, they'd walk away.*

- *Crying means you're weak.*

- *Your pain will make people uncomfortable, so stay silent.*

So, I smiled. And I stayed silent.

☙

A Smile That Should Have Been a Scream

I remember one evening clearly. I was at a gathering with family and friends; the room was full of laughter and conversation. I laughed too—loud, even. Someone turned to me and said, *"You seem to be doing good!"* This was after the passing of my biological mom.

I nodded, my smile wide. But inside, I was crumbling. My chest was tight, my spirit crushed, my heart screaming for relief. Grief was taking me down slowly. I still had unresolved hurt from past trauma, church related hurt, and so on and so forth, but no one seemed to notice.

I should have let the scream out. I should have admitted, I'm hurting. I'm overwhelmed. I don't want to keep pretending.

But instead, I said, *"Yes, God is good"* as If proclaiming that, although He is good, could fill the emptiness silence had carved inside me. I needed to be healed from the inside out that only He could do If I would only admit to the pain.

That night, when everyone else went home, I sat in the quiet and finally let a single tear escape. It rolled down my face like a secret I didn't dare tell anyone.

When Silence Becomes a Prison

☙

Silence felt safe at first. It gave me control. If I didn't speak it, then maybe the pain wasn't real. If I didn't admit it, then no one could use it against me.

But silence is deceptive. It feels like safety until it becomes a prison. And I felt like Paul and Silas I was in the inter most part of the prison of my pain.

Every "I'm fine" was another lock on the door. Every laugh I forced became another brick in the wall. And before long, I was trapped inside my own performance, surrounded by people yet utterly alone.

☙

God in the Silence

In those moments, I didn't realize how near God was. Psalm 34:18 says, *"The Lord is near to the brokenhearted and saves the crushed in spirit."*

He wasn't fooled by my smile. He wasn't offended by my silence. While others saw strength, He saw brokenness. While others heard my laughter, He heard the cries I never uttered.

One night, when the silence felt unbearable, I whispered, *"God, I can't do this anymore."*

And in the stillness, I didn't hear thunder or see a miracle. But I felt His presence—gentle, steady, unshaken by my fragility. He reminded me that silence doesn't scare Him. My broken spirit was not a barrier—it was an invitation for Him to come close.

Reflection

❧

Silence nearly crushed me. But God saved me. He is saving me still.

If you have ever smiled through heartbreak, or laughed while your soul was screaming, hear this: you are not alone. God is nearby. He is not fooled by the mask you wear, and He does not need you to perform strength for Him. He welcomes your tears, your screams, your honesty.

Strength is not pretending. Strength is surrender.

"That silence became the soil where counterfeit love could grow, drawing me into relationships that promised affection but delivered pain."

Time to Journal

What did silence look like for you? What were you afraid that people would see if they looked too closely?

_____

_____

_____

_____

_____

_____

_____

_____

_____

_____

_____

_____

_____

_____

_____

Closing Prayer

ଔ

Father, You see beyond my smile. You know the weight of my silence and the cries I could never put into words. Thank You for being near when my spirit feels crushed and my heart feels hidden. Teach me that strength is not found in silence or pretending, but in surrendering to Your love. I lay down the mask today, and I receive Your healing presence. Draw near to me, Lord, and let my soul find rest in You. In Jesus' name, Amen.

ଔ

Affirmation

I no longer hide my hurt behind a smile. God is near to my brokenness, and His love heals me in silence and in surrender.

Chapter 5: When Grief Shattered My World

The Sting

The Month That Broke Me

☙

There are seasons in life that change you forever. They don't just leave scars — they rewrite the very rhythm of your heartbeat. For me, that month was a storm that ripped through my soul, leaving me standing in the rubble of what I thought my life would be.

It began with a phone call. My phone lit up, and when I saw my sister's name, I answered quickly. I expected to hear her laugh, or a simple *"What are you doing?"* Instead, I heard trembling words: she said that someone called and told her that my nephew had been shot.

Before I could even process, another call came in from a friend, confirming the same devastating truth. My heart dropped. I raced to the emergency room, praying it wasn't real — praying I had misheard.

My nephew. My sweet boy. He wasn't perfect, but he was ours. He was young, still trying to figure life out, still searching for his place. And just like that, he was gone. Stolen by senseless violence. One moment here, the next moment a memory. His absence left a hole in our family that nothing could ever fill. We were still trying to heal from our brother's sudden death in prison and then our mom passing from esophageal cancer. Our family had been torn into pieces and then this.

I felt shattered. Confused. Broken. Why him? Why us? Why now?

And just as I was stumbling under the weight of this loss, I walked into a sterile doctor's office for what I thought would be a routine appointment. The walls were too white, the lights too bright, the air too cold. The doctor's lips moved slowly, but her words cut me open like a knife:

"I'm so sorry. You won't be able to have children."

It was the final blow. One loss after another. One coffin after another. One dream after another buried in the ground. In the same month, I lost the nephew who carried a piece of my heart — the one who was like a son to me — and I lost the children I had prayed my own body would one day carry. My womb was silent. My house was silent. My spirit was silent.

ॐ

Grief in Silence

Grief does not always look like people expect. It doesn't always pour out in tears. Sometimes it comes as a silence so loud it drowns out everything else. A silence that presses on your chest until it feels like you can hardly breathe.

I stopped talking about what I felt. I convinced myself: No one will understand. If you speak it, you'll break. And if you break, you may never recover. So, I wore my smile like a mask. I dressed it up every Sunday morning. I laughed at the right times, hugged when expected, and nodded politely when someone whispered, *"God knows best."*

But behind closed doors, I crumbled. I would lie awake, staring at the ceiling, unable to quiet the storm raging inside. Grief had moved in and made itself at home in my chest. Every breath felt borrowed. Every moment was a battle not to give up completely.

And then came the lies — whispered, subtle, poisonous.

You're broken.

You're unworthy.

You'll never be enough.

If you couldn't protect your nephew, how can you protect anyone?

If you can't have children, what good are you as a wife?

I believed those lies. And in believing them, I made choices I would later regret.

The cycles that I had fought so hard to end came flooding back in my life like they belonged there.

Cycles are sneaky. They don't announce themselves like storms; they slip in like routines. You wake up one day and realize you've been moving in circles, not because you planned to, but because you never stopped to notice the pattern.

For me, my cycle wasn't just about a relationship or a person — it was about me. The rhythm of overcompensating. The grind of proving myself. The silence that swallowed my truth. The fear of slowing down, because if I ever paused, the pain would catch me.

On the outside, I looked like I had it together. On the inside, I was running laps in a prison with no finish line. It was numb but functioning taken to the extreme. I was stuck in survival mode, replaying the same emotional script: **Be strong. Don't cry. Push through. Keep moving**.

But every cycle has an expiration date, and I paid an expensive price before it ended. I reverted back to the only survival mode I knew, the beginning.

೫

The Day I Walked Away

My husband tried. He prayed with me, held me, reminded me that I was still his wife, that my worth was never measured by what I could give him. He begged me to stop speaking divorce into the atmosphere, reminding me that words carry power. And deep down, I knew he was right — God had already taught me the weight of the tongue.

But in my pain, I couldn't hear truth. My heart was numb. My grief couldn't see pass his flaws, my flaws, and what *"should have, could have"* been. My mind was clouded. All I could hear were the accusations of the enemy.

One night, after another silent dinner followed by another argument that wasn't really about what it seemed, something inside of me snapped.

"I can't do this anymore," I whispered, hands trembling as I packed a bag.

I wasn't leaving because I didn't love him. I was leaving because I thought I loved him too much to bind him to my brokenness. I believed he deserved a wife who could give him children, a future, a legacy. I thought I was sparing him.

But in truth, I was running. Running from pain I didn't know how to carry. Running from the silence that haunted me. Running from myself. Running from that nine-year-old little girl inside of me.

And so, I walked out. Eventually, I signed the papers and ended the marriage. The covenant I had vowed to honor until death — I tore apart with my own hands. I thought I was saving him, but in reality, I was destroying us both.

The silence in my home became unbearable. I had lost my nephew. I had lost the dream of children. And now, I had divorced the man I once believed I would grow old with. I was alive, but it felt as if I had died too. The agony and pain of it all almost cost me my sanity.

☙

When God Whispered in the Dark

For six to eight long months, I barely heard anything from anyone. Friends fell silent. Family didn't know what to say. Worst of all, it felt as if even God was silent.

During that time, I was deployed in Texas working as an insurance adjuster, and one evening, my roommate told me her husband was coming to visit, so I'd have the room to myself. That night, as the door closed behind me, the silence pressed in again.

I whispered into the emptiness: *"God, where are You? Don't You see me? Don't You care? How could you let me lose everything?"*

Then something shifted. An overwhelming presence filled the room, rushing over me like a flood. I fell to my knees and began to weep, worship, and pour out every burden I had carried in silence. For the first time in months, my lips opened in prayer.

And in the middle of my tears, I heard it — not with my ears, but in the depths of my spirit. A whisper, soft yet thunderous:

"Behold, I am doing a new thing. Do you not see it? Even in this desert, I will make rivers flow." (Isaiah 43:19)

At first, I resisted. How could new life spring up in the shadow of so much death? How could good possibly be born from a barren womb and a broken heart? Yet the whisper kept coming, like waves upon the shore, steady and unrelenting.

It wasn't an instant miracle. I didn't wake up the next morning completely healed. But something within me begin to pivot. A seed of hope was planted in the dry ground of my soul. God was inviting me into something new — a pivot I didn't even know I needed.

"Therefore, if anyone is in Christ, he is a new creation. The old has passed away; behold, the new has come." (2 Corinthians 5:17)

෴

The Pivot

A pivot is a shift. A turn. A moment where your direction changes permanently. For me, that pivot wasn't about me finally being strong enough to choose or think differently. It was about God being strong enough to pull me out.

That month could have ended me. In some ways, it did. It ended the version of me who believed she had to control everything, who wore strength like armor, who thought her worth depended on keeping everyone else happy.

Grief tore through me, but it also broke me open. And in that breaking, I could finally hear God's whisper. His voice became my anchor: "I am doing a new thing."

I didn't know what that *"new thing"* would look like. I didn't know if I would ever become whole again. I didn't know if my marriage could be restored. I didn't know if the ache in my chest would ever fully fade.

But I began to believe. I began to hope. And I whispered the only *"yes"* I could manage — a trembling yes to the possibility that God's plan for me was not finished.

That was my pivot.

☙

What Grief Has Taught Me

As I walked through the valley of loss, God began to teach me lessons I would carry for the rest of my journey:

- Grief reveals love. The deeper the pain, the greater the love that was shared. My husband was God's love for me in human form.
- My tears for my nephew were not weakness — they were love in liquid form.
- My womb does not define my worth. I had believed the lie that motherhood was the only way to be whole, the only way to leave a legacy. God reminded me that He had called me to birth more than children — He had called me to birth purpose, vision, and life into others.

- Isolation is a trap. The enemy wanted me silent, hidden, and alone. But God created us for community, for connection, for love. Even in my silence, He was gently drawing me out, reminding me that His presence would never leave me.

Grief broke me, yes. But it also positioned me. It stripped away the surface, so God could heal the deepest, darkest, and hardest parts of me. Sometimes, the breaking is not the end — it's the beginning of becoming.

Grief left me broken, silenced, and alone. But it also cracked me wide open, making room for God to pour His love into me. What I thought was the end was actually the beginning of something sacred. Out of my wilderness, He was leading me into a place I never expected — a place where true healing would finally begin.

I want to pause here for more reflection, mainly because grief almost paralyzed me and I didn't realize it until it had snuck upon me. If you are someone you know is dealing with uncontrollable grief, please seek help from a trusted voice in your life or a professional.

☙

Reflection

This chapter reminds us that grief is not a weakness — it is evidence of love. Loss has a way of shaking us to the core, stripping away our illusions of control and exposing the places where our hearts ache the most. In those silent seasons when God seems far away, we often hear the loudest lies of the enemy: *"You're not enough. You'll never heal. You've lost everything."*

But grief, as heavy as it is, can become holy ground. It humbles us. It empties us. It positions us to hear God's whisper. And when He speaks — even in the silence — His Word carries life. His promise in Isaiah still stands: "Behold, I am doing a new thing."

What we thought was the end can become the doorway into something new. Out of the ashes, God brings beauty. Out of barrenness, He brings fruit. Out of silence, He speaks.

ଓଃ

Key Take Away

- Grief is proof of love. The pain you feel reveals how deeply you cared. Don't despise your tears — they are a testament to the bond you shared.

- Your worth is not defined by loss. Whether by what you can or cannot give, your identity is secure in Christ, not in circumstances.

- Silence is not abandonment. Even when God seems quiet, He is present, listening, and working in ways you cannot yet see.

- There is purpose in the breaking. What feels like the end may actually be God preparing you for a new beginning.

Let's Journal

ॐ

Think back to a season of deep grief in your own life.

- What loss shook you to your core?
- How did you cope — or avoid coping?
- How did grief affect your relationships with others and with God?

As you reflect, ask yourself: Can I see now how God was planting seeds in the very soil of my sorrow? Write what comes to your heart, without judgment.

_____

_____

_____

_____

_____

_____

_____

_____

_____

_____

_____

Closing Prayer

ଔ

Father, I bring You my broken pieces. You see the nights I cried silently, the days I smiled while crumbling inside. You know the dreams I buried, the people I lost, the pain I carried, and the disappointments that weighed me down. Today, I lay it all at Your feet. Lord, do what only You can do — breathe life into the places that feel dead. Let living water flow through my desert. Heal me. Restore me. Remind me that You are doing a new thing in me. Amen.

ଔ

Affirmation

Even in my deepest grief, I am not forgotten. My pain does not define me, my womb does not limit me, and my losses do not diminish me. God is birthing new purpose in me, and His living water flows through every dry place in my soul. I am becoming whole, I am becoming new, and I will rise again.

Chapter 6: Where Healing Began

As I reached out to God, God continued to heal me. The healing room wasn't a physical place at first — it was a posture of surrender. I came to a moment in my life when survival was no longer enough. I had learned how to smile through pain, how to keep moving even when my soul was fractured, how to perform strength while my heart silently bled. But something shifted. I reached the end of what pretending could fix.

Healing didn't start loud; it started quietly. It started with accountability, it started with obeying the instruction given to me by my leader, it started on the floor, with tear-stained pillows and whispered prayers. It started with me finally saying out loud, *"I'm not okay."* And for the first time, I didn't try to fix it on my own. For once I stopped being strong and I allowed God to strengthen me from the inside out, this was my time to heal for real, this was just me and Jesus.

☙

The Hard Work of Being Whole

Healing is not for the faint of heart. It's not all oil and altar calls. It's not all pretty prayers or instant deliverance. For me it was showing up to therapy sessions either in person or via phone, it was following the instructions that my leader was giving me when my instinct was saying run. It was journaling through memories I swore I would never touch again. It was learning to be honest with myself after years of silence and self-protection

The healing room became my sacred space — sometimes it was counsel, sometimes my prayer closet, sometimes just a quiet corner where I could breathe again without the weight of performing strength. Sometimes it was relapsing into old thought patterns and then coming to myself and snapping back out of it, renewed and refreshed by a word from God.

☙

Unlearning Survival

For years, I wore survival like a badge of honor. I knew how to get through, how to carry the load, how to be the strong one. But survival is not the same as wholeness. Healing required me to put down the armor that once kept me safe but now kept me bound.

I had to learn how to receive love again — not the kind I had to earn, but the kind that was freely given. I had to forgive myself for what I thought healing "should've" looked like. I had to accept that progress doesn't always feel like victory. Sometimes it feels like crying through another session, writing another page in my journal, or sitting in silence while God mended the pieces I couldn't touch.

༄

Heaven Met Me There

Every time I showed up in that space, Heaven met me there. I didn't always feel fire or see visions. Sometimes it was just the gentle whisper of God saying, *"I'm here."*

God didn't rush my healing. He sat with me in it. He taught me that broken pieces don't disqualify me — they invite Him in. The same hands that formed me were now binding up what life had shattered. And slowly, light began to break through the cracks. I could breathe. Day by day the father began to make me whole.

༄

Becoming Whole on Purpose

Wholeness isn't something you stumble into. It's intentional. It's deciding to no longer live from the wound but from the healed place. It's letting go of what no longer serves your soul and making room for what restores it.

I became consistent — not perfect, but present. Prayer became more honest. Accountability became less scary. Journaling became my release valve. And day by day, the woman who once lived in fragments began to rise in fullness.

༺ ༻

My Breakthrough Moment

There was one night in particular when I walked into my healing room heavy — the kind of heavy words that can't explain. I had cried, wrestled, and almost given up. But in that quiet space, I felt God say, *"Daughter, it's safe now. You don't have to carry it anymore."* Listening to that talk with Gid freed me in a way that I can't explain. I no longer had to fear what others thought or what they knew. God was freeing me and who the Son set free is free indeed John 8:36.

Something broke in me that night. Not in a way that destroyed me — in a way that set me free. Healing didn't erase my past, but it removed its grip from my present.

Healing didn't just change how I felt — it changed how I saw myself. The woman who once tiptoed around her pain began to walk boldly in purpose. In the stillness of that room, I didn't just find peace; I found me. But healing isn't a finish line — it's a doorway. And on the other side of that doorway was a new chapter of becoming, of walking in the strength I once only prayed for. I was no longer fighting to survive. I was learning to live.

Closing Prayer

☙

Father, thank You for meeting me in the room where my pain lived. Thank You for teaching me that healing isn't weakness — it's warfare. Help me to keep showing up, even when it's uncomfortable. Bind up every wound and breathe life into every broken place. Make me whole from the inside out. In Jesus' name, amen.

Affirmation

☙

I give myself permission to heal. I am no longer surviving — I am becoming whole.

Chapter 7: Forgiveness Ain't Weakness

"Bear with each other and forgive one another if any of you has a grievance against someone. Forgive as the Lord forgave you."

— *Colossians 3:13*

The Apologized Pain

ଔ

Forgiveness has a way of humbling you. It isn't soft. It isn't easy. And it most definitely isn't weak. Forgiveness is the quiet kind of strength that makes the enemy nervous — because it breaks chains that pain tried to keep locked.

For years, I carried a weight that wasn't mine to bear. It sat heavy in the quiet places of my soul — heavy on my shoulders almost as if it belonged there. The kind of pain that didn't scream anymore but whispered just enough to remind me it was still a part of me. I waited for an apology that never came. I hoped for a moment of acknowledgment that was never given.

But the truth is, forgiveness isn't about the other person. It's about setting yourself free.

ଔ

The Person I Had to Forgive

There's a kind of hurt that runs deep — the kind that steals innocence and buries trust under layers of silence. I had to forgive the ones who abused me. Not because they earned it. Not because it didn't matter. But because holding on to it was slowly suffocating the woman I was becoming.

I kept waiting for the day they would say, *"I'm sorry."* It never came. There were plenty of opportunities but neither took it, and that was when I finally learned something sacred — closure doesn't always come wrapped in an apology. Sometimes closure is you, standing in your healing, deciding that their silence will not hold your voice hostage any longer.

Forgiveness wasn't a moment; it was a process. It was me peeling back the layers of pain, fear, and shame, and finally saying, *"You don't get to own this part of me anymore."*

☙

The Hardest Forgiveness: Myself

Forgiving them was hard. But forgiving myself was even harder.

I had to forgive the little girl who thought it was her fault. The young woman who carried shame that was never hers to carry. The woman who struggled to trust, love, and let people in because of the damage that was done to her.

I had to look at myself in the mirror and say, *"You didn't deserve what happened to you. But you do deserve to be healed."*

This was the turning point — not when they changed, but when I did. Forgiveness didn't excuse the wrong. It released me from its grip. And for the first time, it felt good to live without the guilt.

☙

A Different Kind of Freedom

The day I chose to forgive wasn't dramatic. It was quiet, almost sacred. It was the day I laid the weight down and picked up my peace.

I realized that forgiveness is not weakness — it is strength clothed in grace. It's choosing to rise even when the apology never comes. It's saying, *"I won't let bitterness rewrite my story."*

The apology I never received no longer has power over me. Forgiveness gave me back myself.

Forgiveness didn't just set me free from what happened — it cleared the fog that kept me from truly seeing myself. For so long, the pain, shame, and silence distorted the reflection staring back at me. But once I laid the weight down, I could finally look in the mirror without flinching. For the first time, I didn't just see a woman who survived. I saw a woman becoming whole — worthy, loved, and enough.

Journaling Prompt

ଓଃ

Who have you forgiven that never apologized — and what changed in you afterward?

Write their name, renounce the act(s), release the pain, and remind yourself: forgiveness isn't about them. It's about your healing.

_____

_____

_____

_____

_____

_____

_____

_____

_____

_____

_____

_____

_____

Closing Prayer

❧

"Lord, teach me to forgive the way You forgave me — fully, freely, and without conditions."

Heavenly Father,

Today, I release the weight of every unspoken apology. I lay down the anger, the silence, the ache that has lingered too long. I forgive not because it was fair, but because I refuse to stay bound to what tried to break me.

I forgive the one who hurt me. I forgive the ones who stayed silent. And I forgive myself — for the years I carried shame, for the moments I believed the lie that it was my fault.

Lord, heal the hidden places that forgiveness touches. Fill the empty spaces with Your love. Let my forgiveness be a weapon that breaks generational chains and ushers in freedom for me and those who will follow after me.

In Jesus' Name, Amen.

Affirmation of Freedom

❧

"Forgiveness is not weakness — it is strength wrapped in grace."

- *I choose to forgive even when the apology never comes.*
- *I choose peace over bitterness.*
- *I choose healing over holding on.*
- *I forgive myself for what was never mine to carry.*
- *I am free. I am whole. I am walking in peace.*

Chapter 8: The Woman in the Mirror — Seeing My Self-Worth

"I praise You because I am fearfully and wonderfully made; Your works are wonderful, I know that full well." — Psalm 139:14

Looking in the Mirror for Real

༒

There came a moment when forgiveness wasn't just something I prayed through — it became the lens through which I finally saw myself clearly.

For years, I stood in front of the mirror but didn't truly see the woman staring back at me. All I could see was the pain, the shame, and the stories others wrote on my heart. I saw what I had survived but not who I had become. My reflection had become a silent reminder of everything I endured, not everything I am.

But after laying the weight down, the fog began to lift. And what stood before me wasn't a broken woman trying to piece herself together anymore. It was a woman becoming whole. A woman learning to love the reflection that once made her flinch. A woman stepping into her worth, not because of what she survived, but because of who she is.

༒

For So Long, I Couldn't See Me

There was a time when the mirror was my enemy. I avoided my reflection because I didn't like the woman looking back at me. She carried too much — pain, guilt, silence, and scars. I could see what life had done to me, but I couldn't see what God had placed inside of me.

I believed the lies whispered by trauma — that I was too damaged, too unworthy, too broken to ever truly be loved or seen. I let rejection, abandonment, and abuse speak louder than the truth of God's voice.

But the thing about mirrors is this: they don't lie. They reflect what is. The problem was never the mirror — it was my vision. I had been looking through pain instead of promise. Through scars instead of strength. Through shame instead of worth. And what I saw was that little girl still hurt, broken. Confused and silent.

The day I faced the mirror without the weight of unforgiveness was the day I began to see me again.

ଔ

Learning to Love the Reflection

Learning to love myself wasn't instant. It was a daily decision — some days quiet and confident, other days shaky and tear-filled. I had to speak to the woman in the mirror the way God spoke to me: with grace, with truth, with love.

I stood there and declared over myself:

"You are not what they did to you. You are not the mistakes you made. You are not the shame you carried. You are His masterpiece."

And slowly, I stopped shrinking in the reflection. Slowly, my shoulders straightened. My head lifted. My eyes held more light than pain.

This was the woman God saw all along — the woman who was hidden beneath fear and hurt. She had always been there. I just needed to give myself permission to see her too.

ଔ

My Worth Is Not Negotiable

There was a season when I gave my worth away like it was up for discussion. I let people define me, minimize me, break me, and silence me. But true healing taught me this: my worth is not negotiable.

The woman in the mirror is not a project. She is a promise.

She is not something to be fixed — she is someone to be honored.

She is not defined by the scars — she is defined by the strength that came through them.

My reflection no longer makes me flinch. It makes me stand taller. Because when you know who you are in God, no one can convince you that you are less than.

☙

The Healing in the Mirror

The mirror became my safe place — not because it changed, but because I did. I stopped seeing a victim and started seeing a victor. I stopped seeing a wounded girl and started seeing a healed woman.

And here's the truth: healing doesn't make the past disappear. It removes its power to distort your view of who you are.

I'm not who I was when the pain happened. I'm not even who I was yesterday. I am becoming more of the woman God created me to be — bold, beautiful, and whole.

The woman in the mirror finally looks back at me with confidence. Not because life didn't hurt me, but because grace rebuilt me.

Seeing myself clearly in the mirror was more than a moment of healing — it was a declaration of war against everything that once tried to silence me. When I finally recognized my worth, I also realized something greater: my story wasn't meant to end with me. The same pain that once crushed me was now becoming the very platform God would use to set others free. I will never be silent again. My scars no longer whispered shame; they began to speak strength. And the woman in the mirror was no longer just a survivor — she was a weapon.

There's a moment in every healing journey when pain stops being the loudest voice in the room. It doesn't happen overnight. It happens after the tears, after the prayers that had no words, after the silent nights where you wondered if the pieces of your heart would ever fit again.

And then... something shifts. What once broke you no longer holds you hostage. What once silenced you now gives you language.

I've learned that wounds don't just leave scars—they leave stories. And when those stories are surrendered to God, they stop being evidence of what was lost and become proof of what was overcome. The very thing the enemy thought would take you out becomes the weapon God uses to shake someone else free.

There was a time when my testimony felt too heavy to speak. But now, I understand—it was never meant to stay buried in my chest. It was meant to be carried into rooms, whispered to the broken, shouted in victory, and lived out loud so others could see that healing is real.

This next chapter isn't about pain—it's about power. It's about the holy exchange when wounds turn into weapons, silence turns into testimony, and survival turns into purpose.

ଓ

🙏 Prayer/Declaration

"Father, thank You for trusting me with a story that once felt too painful to carry. Today, I declare that my scars are no longer symbols of shame but weapons of victory. Use my testimony to break chains, heal hearts, and remind someone that You still redeem, restore, and resurrect what's been broken. Let my life be proof that what tried to destroy me has now been disarmed. In Jesus' name, amen."

Journaling Prompt

ঔ

What do you see when you look in the mirror — and what truth does God say about you that your pain used to drown out?

Write it down. Speak it out loud. Remind your reflection that she is more than what happened to her. She is who God says she is.

_____
_____
_____
_____
_____
_____
_____
_____
_____
_____
_____
_____
_____

Closing Prayer

ରେ

"Lord, help me to see myself the way You see me — loved, chosen, and whole."

Heavenly Father,

Thank You for opening my eyes to the woman in the mirror. For so long I only saw pain, but now I see purpose. I thank You for reminding me that I am fearfully and wonderfully made — not because of what I've done, but because of who You are in me.

Help me to silence every lie that tells me I am not enough. Remind me daily of my worth. Let my reflection be a reminder of Your grace, not my pain. Thank You for restoring the woman I stopped seeing.

In Jesus' Name, Amen.

ରେ

Affirmation of Worth

- *"I am not my past — I am God's masterpiece."*
- *I choose to see myself the way God sees me.*
- *I am worthy of love, healing, and purpose.*
- *I am becoming everything I was created to be.*
- *I am more than my scars.*
- *I am whole. I am beautiful. I am enough.*

Chapter 9: From Wound to Weapon

"They overcame him by the blood of the Lamb and by the word of their testimony."

— *Revelation 12:11*

There comes a point in your healing where the pain that once tried to bury you can no longer keep you silent. It doesn't happen all at once. It happens after the tears. After the quiet nights. After the conversations with God that no one else heard. It happens when the weight you've carried finally shifts from being a burden to becoming a weapon.

I've learned that the enemy doesn't just attack because of where you are — he attacks because of what's in you. His job is to come in and try to steal kill and destroy. He knows that if you ever stop bleeding in silence and start speaking with power, lives will be changed. He knows that if you ever step out of the shadows and say, "Yes, this happened to me, but God healed me," then strongholds will break. And for a long time, I let my pain hush my voice. I let shame convince me that my story was too messy to be used. The devil was betting on me going through so much that he would forever keep me silent,

But God has a way of rewriting what hell tried to destroy. The very places I tried to hide became the places He used to reach others. The wounds became the weapon.

༺ ༻

Pain That Speaks

There was a time when my pain spoke through silence. I smiled while I was bleeding. I encouraged others while secretly trying to hold myself together. I showed up strong when I was falling apart inside. And for a long time, I thought survival was enough. But survival without healing isn't freedom.

When I finally started to heal, my pain started to speak differently. No longer as a cry from a broken place, but as a testimony from a healed one. That's the thing about pain that's been surrendered to God — it begins to prophesy. It begins to declare victory where the enemy thought there would only be defeat. It becomes a sound that hell can't silence.

Turning Pain into Purpose

☙

Purpose is rarely born in comfort. It's forged in fire. It's refined in places where everything in you wants to give up but God whispers, "Not yet." And when you finally rise, there's a different kind of authority in your voice — not because you read about it, but because you lived through it.

I'll never forget the first time someone looked me in the eyes and said, "Your testimony gave me hope." In that moment, it hit me: what tried to destroy me had just been used to strengthen someone else. The very thing I once questioned — the pain I tried to bury — had become a tool in God's hand. I didn't have to be perfect. I just had to be available.

That's the power of testimony. It reaches places that rehearsed speeches never will. It speaks to the heart, not the surface. It shows people that God still moves in real lives, not just in Bible stories.

☙

When My Story Unlocked Someone Else's Freedom

I once shared a piece of my testimony with someone who was silently carrying the kind of pain I used to know too well. I didn't sugarcoat it. I didn't wrap it up with pretty bows. I simply told the truth — about the darkness, the brokenness, and the God who met me there. Though the enemy wanted me to be ashamed, the word of God reminded me in the word not to fear man or their faces.

Tears began to fall from their eyes. They said, "I thought I was the only one. I thought God couldn't use me after what I've been through." But in that moment, something shifted. Chains started to break — not because of me, but because of the power of a word spoken from a healed place. Had I disobeyed God the person never would have had the courage to break free.

That's when I realized... my story was never meant to stay buried in my chest. It was meant to breathe. It was meant to reach. It was meant to free. It was meant to help, and I couldn't worry about who would be mad or offended because I told my truth.

ଓ

Testimony Is a Weapon

There is nothing more dangerous to the enemy than a believer who refuses to be silent. Testimony carries weight in the Spirit. It declares, *"The enemy tried it, but God won."* It reminds hell that no matter how hard it hit, it couldn't take you out.

When you open your mouth and speak from a healed place, you snatch victory from the enemy's hands and hand it back to God. Your story becomes a weapon — not a weapon that wounds others, but a weapon that destroys lies, breaks shame, and unlocks hope.

Journaling Prompt:

ଓ

How is your story a weapon in someone else's battle? Reflect on the parts of your journey God has redeemed and how He can use those same places to strengthen others.

_____

_____

_____

_____

_____

_____

_____

_____

_____

_____

_____

_____

_____

_____

Declaration Prayer

☙

Father, thank You for trusting me with a story that once felt too painful to speak. Thank You for turning what was meant to break me into a weapon that builds others. Today I declare that my scars no longer symbolize shame — they testify of victory. Use my voice, my pain, and my journey to set captives free and remind the enemy that he lost. Let my story carry Your glory. In Jesus' name, amen.

Chapter 10: I'm Not Who I Was

"Therefore, if anyone is in Christ, he is a new creation; the old has passed away; behold, the new has come."

— *2 Corinthians 5:17*

There comes a moment when your soul exhales. When you realize you've survived what was designed to break you — and not only survived but outlived it. For years, I walked through seasons with wounds still bleeding, carrying weights that God never asked me to carry. I thought healing meant pretending I was okay. But true healing came when I stopped performing strength and actually became strong. When I got tired of letting my past dictate how my present and future would be.

I am not who I was. I no longer walk with the language of pain — I walk with the voice of power. This is no longer a story of what I lost; this is the story of how God restored, redeemed, and rebuilt me.

The woman writing these words is not a victim. She is a victor. A warrior. A healed woman who's learned that God can take the same pain that once buried you and use it as the foundation you stand on. I've fought through dark nights, grief so heavy it suffocated me, and cycles that tried to convince me that broken was all I'd ever be. But today, I stand free.

☙

No More Cycles

No more mind battles! I made a decision: I will not repeat what God has already broken. No more circling the same mountains. No more entertaining what wounded me. No more shrinking to make room for pain that no longer belongs.

This next season of my life is marked by clarity. I've learned that grief may visit, but it no longer gets to live here. Pain may knock, but it no longer gets a seat at my table. The cycles that once controlled my life have been interrupted — not by my own strength, but by the power of God.

I've walked through enough wilderness to know the sound of freedom. I've buried old versions of me that were never meant to survive this far.

This is not survival anymore... this is thriving. This is me walking in peace, in purpose, and in promise.

※

No More Carrying the Grief

Grief is real, and for a long time it wrapped itself around my identity. I grieved what was taken, what I lost, what should've been, and what I thought I'd never have again. But grief is not my forever. It was a chapter, not the whole book.

I've learned to honor what happened without becoming trapped in it and without being bitter. To feel it, release it, and let God fill the places it once occupied. I am no longer walking with invisible weight on my shoulders. I'm walking with a crown. I'm walking in freedom.

The woman I am today does not apologize for healing. She does not apologize for joy. She does not apologize for outgrowing what once held her down.

※

Becoming Her

I look in the mirror now and I see a woman I once prayed to become. She's softer, but she's stronger. She's more grounded, more rooted in God. She no longer hides behind walls of defense, introvertness, or fear. She doesn't chase love out of desperation; she waits for love out of wholeness.

I believe in love again. I believe in marriage again. Not as an escape from pain, but as an extension of promise. I see myself loving freely — not from a fractured heart, but from a healed one. Will love "spin the block"? If so, this time love won't find me broken... it will find me whole.

God is writing a new chapter for me — one where I love from a pure and safe place. A marriage where I don't have walls up; and when that day comes – it won't be me begging to be seen... it'll be me already standing in the light.

పఠ

Victor, Not Victim

For years, I carried the names life gave me — I felt abandoned, unwanted, unworthy, too broken to be loved. Never accepting the love that was given to me. But now I wear the name redeemed. I wear the name chosen. I wear the name healed.

I no longer carry the weight of old labels. I no longer walk in shame. I am not what happened to me. I am not the mistakes I made. I am what God spoke over me.

I am proof that healing is possible. I am evidence that cycles can be broken. I am a living testimony that what the enemy meant for evil, God has turned for good.

A Letter to the Woman Still Healing

ଔ

To the woman who will read these words in her own dark night... I see you. I may not know your name, but I know that feeling of being stuck between what broke you and who you're trying to become.

I need you to know — this is not the end. God is not done with you. You will not carry this grief forever. You will not live in this cycle forever. You will not cry these same tears forever. One day, you will breathe again and it won't hurt to do so. One day, you will smile and it won't be forced. One day, love will hold you gently, and your heart will not flinch.

Your story will not end in pain — it will rise in purpose. You are not broken beyond repair. You are being rebuilt for glory.

To the woman reading these words with tears forming in the corners of your eyes...

To the woman who has carried more than she could ever explain...

To the woman who learned silence long before she learned safety...

To the woman who survived what should have broken her...

I want you to know this:

You are not alone.

I know what it feels like to be touched too soon, too young, too wrong.

I know what it feels like to be separated from the mother you needed,

to grow up hungry for love,

hungry for belonging,

hungry for truth

that no one ever gave you.

I know what it feels like to search for pieces of yourself in people who were never built to hold you...

to crave affection from places that only left you emptier...

to stay silent because silence felt safer than speaking.

I know what it feels like to be told lies about who you are,

to be shaped by trauma that tried to bury your identity,

to exist in a story that you didn't choose.

But sis — hear me clearly:

Your trauma is not your identity.

Your past is not your prison.

Your wounds are not your worth.

You are a woman who survived.

A woman who endured.

A woman who is still standing.

And anything that is still standing

can rise.

There is nothing you've experienced that God cannot redeem.

Nothing taken that He cannot restore.

Nothing broken that He cannot breathe life into again.

Your voice is coming back.

Your identity is being rebuilt.

Your heart is learning how to trust its own beating again.

I want you to know…

What happened to you was not your fault.

What they did to you did not diminish your purpose.

What you lost will not compare to what God restores.

You have permission to heal.

You have permission to speak.

You have permission to break cycles that ended generations before you.

You have permission to become the woman your younger self needed.

If no one ever told you:

I see you.

I honor your journey.

I believe your story.

I celebrate your survival.

And I am standing with you —

not as someone who escaped pain untouched,

but as someone who walked through the fire

and came out rebuilt.

You are worthy of love that lasts.

You are worthy of peace that stays.

You are worthy of joy that doesn't hurt.

You are worthy of wholeness without apology.

Your story does not end in the wound.

It ends in the healing.

And woman to woman, heart to heart —

I pray that you rise,

not in the shadow of what happened,

but in the fullness of who God says you are.

You will tell your story with boldness not bitterness.

ॐ

With love, strength, and sisterhood,

Dr. Kimberly Lowe

Journaling Prompt

ଔ

What would you say to the younger version of yourself — the one who didn't see this moment coming? Speak to her from your healed place. Tell her she made it. Tell her she's safe now.

_____

_____

_____

_____

_____

_____

_____

_____

_____

_____

_____

_____

_____

_____

Declaration

☙

I am not who I was.

I am not bound to what tried to bury me.

I am not stuck in cycles I've outgrown.

I am not carrying grief I've already laid at the altar.

I am healed.

I am whole.

I am free.

I choose to love again. I choose to trust again. I choose to live again. I walk boldly into the future God has written for me — not as a victim of pain, but as a victor in promise.

☙

Prayer

"*Father, thank You for closing this chapter with victory. Thank You for breaking the cycles that once held me, for lifting the weight of grief, and for teaching me that I was never meant to stay in the valley. I give You my past — all of it — and I step fully into the future You've written. I declare that this next season will be marked by joy, love, purpose, and divine alignment. Let my life continue to be proof that You redeem and restore all things. In Jesus' name, amen.*"

Final Word

I am not the woman who walked through the fire.

I am the woman who came out shining.

I am not what I lost.

I am what God redeemed.

No more chains.

No more cycles.

No more carrying grief that does not belong to me.

This is not my ending.

This is my becoming.

This is my beginning.

The old has passed away.

And what stands here now... is a healed, whole, and unshakable woman of purpose.

I AM FREE

I AM READY FOR MY NEXT

I EMBRACE NEW OPPORTUNITIES AND COLABORATIONS

I AM HEALED

ABOUT THE AUTHOR

Dr. Kimberly Lowe is a spirit-led author, speaker, and life coach who transforms pain into purpose with boldness and grace.

A visionary and seer, she has been walking with God since childhood, carrying a prophetic voice that speaks healing into the hearts of those bound by grief, trauma, and broken relationships.

As the founder of **Back to Life Consulting Services**, she specializes in coaching individuals through singleness, marriage, and loss—equipping them to rise with clarity and confidence.

Her books are soul-deep journeys filled with spiritual insight, raw truth, and redemptive power.

Whether on the page or the pulpit, Dr. Kimberly brings divine wisdom wrapped in elegance, compassion, and courage.

ZOE LIFE CCP

Zoë Life Coaching, Consulting, & Publishing is a publishing imprint that is dedicated to unlocking the full potential of individuals. Our expertise includes life coaching to empower personal growth, literary coaching to nurture writing talents and publishing skills, and comprehensive literary publishing services.

Scan the QR code below to visit our website today view our catalogue and services.

www.ingramcontent.com/pod-product-compliance
Lightning Source LLC
Chambersburg PA
CBHW050656160426
43194CB00010B/1968